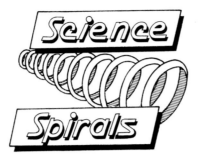

In the Air

Julie Fitzpatrick
Illustrated by Sara Silcock

Silver Burdett Company
Morristown, New Jersey

Library of Congress Cataloging in Publication Data

Fitzpatrick, Julie.
    In the air.

    (Science spirals)
    Includes index.
    Summary: Gives instructions for making several kinds
of objects to sail or glide in the wind and demonstrate
the basic principles of flight.
    1. Flight — Juvenile literature. 2. Paper airplanes —
Juvenile literature. [1. Air — Experiments. 2. Flight.
3. Paper airplanes. 4. Experiments] I. Silcock, Sara,
ill. II. Title. III. Series: Fitzpatrick, Julie.
Science spirals.
TL547.F48   1985   629.132'3'076   84-40839
ISBN 0-382-09060-8

First published in Great Britain in 1984 by
Hamish Hamilton Children's Books
Garden House, 57-59 Long Acre, London WC2E 9J2

Copyright © 1984 by Julie Fitzpatrick (text)
Copyright © 1984 by Sara Silcock (illustrations)
All Rights Reserved

Designed by Linda Rogers Associates

Adapted and published in the United States, 1985, by
Silver Burdett Company, Morristown, N.J.

ISBN 0-382-09060-8

Library of Congress Catalog Card No. 84-40839

Introduction

Have you watched birds fly, and jet planes roaring through the sky? Have you wondered how things stay up in the air? Have you wanted to know how to make a kite or a glider that will sail in the wind?

Here is a book that will show you how to make several kinds of things to sail or glide in the wind. It will also show you how to propel things through the air. Now all you have to do is wait for a windy day to try out your own experiments in the air.

Remember

Always launch your flying things
in an open space.
Make sure that you are away
from roads, buildings, and trees.

Equipment you need for experiments in this book

Paper
Cardboard
Pencils
Rulers
Scissors
Tape
Clay
Feathers, milk bottle tops
Black plastic trash bag
2 sticks
2 plastic shopping bags
String
Wire coat-hanger
2 corks
A small toy to be a
    parachute person
Some long balloons
A balloon pump
A bulldog clip
Some drinking straws
Paper clips
Oaktag

In the Air

Go outside on a windy day.
What things can you see
moving in the air?
Are the trees moving?
Can you see pieces of paper
or leaves being blown about?
Can you feel the wind
blowing your hair and
your clothes?

3

Air is all around us.
Air that is moving is
called wind.
What happens to things in
the air on a windy day?

Take some of these things
outside with you.
Let each one go into
the air.
Which way do they fly?
Do they turn in the air?
Do they fall to the
ground quickly or slowly?

How to make Flying Tails

You need ★ a piece of plastic
(a trash bag will do)
★ a stick
★ tape

Cut the plastic into thin tails
about 1 yard long.
Hold the tails at one end and
tape them together.
Now tape them to the top
of the stick.
Take the stick outside on
a windy day.
How can you move the stick
so that the tails fly up
in the air?

What happens when you pull a bag through the air?

Make a bag-on-a-stick like this.

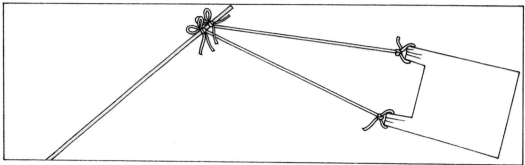

You need ★ a plastic shopping   ★ a long stick
bag   ★ some string

Cut two pieces of string
each measuring 30 inches long.
Tie the bag to the stick
like this.
Take the bag outside on
a windy day.

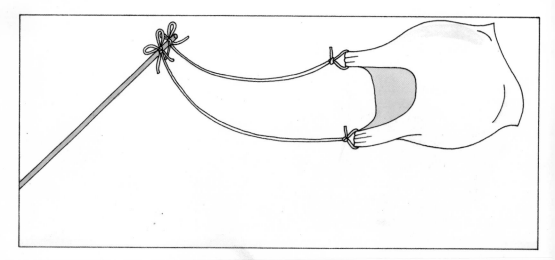

Put your back to the wind and
hold the stick so that air
can rush into the bag.
What happens to the bag?

Keep pulling the stick
towards you.
Does the bag come
towards you easily?

What can you feel that is
pushing it back?

Air that is moving can
lift things and hold them up.
It can make a kite fly.

How to make your own kite

You need ★ A thin wire coat-
hanger (ask an adult to
cut off the hook part)
★ a plastic shopping
bag
★ some thin string

★ 3 strips of
plastic
to make the tail.
Each one should
measure about
5 feet long
★ tape

Pull the coat-hanger out
all around until it makes
a shape like this.
Put the coat hanger on a
piece of plastic and
trim around the edges.
Fold the plastic over
the wire and tape the tail
to the bottom of the kite.

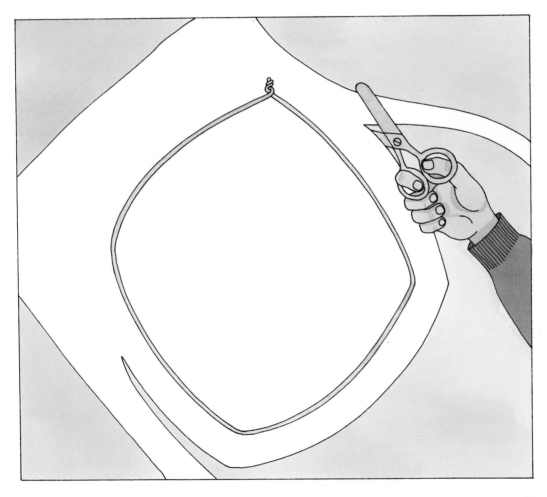

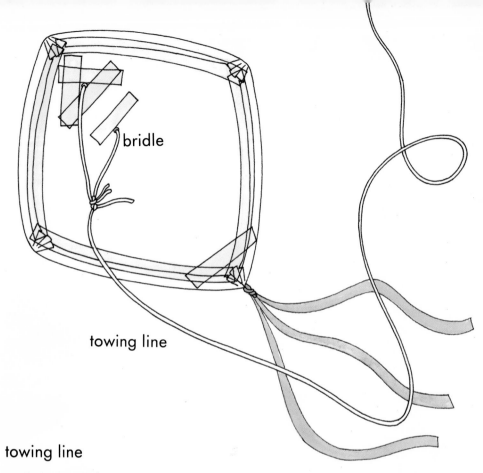

bridle

towing line

towing line

Ask an adult to help you make
two holes in the plastic.
Thread a piece of string
through the holes.
Make the kite stronger
by putting tape around the holes.
Tie the ends together at
the back of the kite.
This is called the bridle.
Tie a long piece of string
to the middle of the bridle.
This piece of string is
called the towing line.

Stand with your back to
the wind and hold the
towing line.
Ask a friend to hold the
kite up high.
The kite must be tilted
towards you.
Then the wind can get
underneath the kite to
lift it up.
Remember how your bag-
on-a-stick was lifted
up in the air.

Gently pull the kite
towards you.
Does this help it to
go up higher?

What happens if you let paper fall through the air?

Get two pieces of paper of the same size.
Crumple one piece into a ball.
Hold one piece of paper in each hand.
Which do you think will land first?

Let both pieces go at the same time.
Which piece of paper fell more slowly?

Do this lots of times.
Does the same one always land first?
How does the sheet of paper fall?
How is this different from the way in which the ball of paper falls?

Get two corks of the same size.
Drop one cork through the air.

What could you fasten to
the cork to slow it down?
A piece of paper stuck on
top of the cork might work.

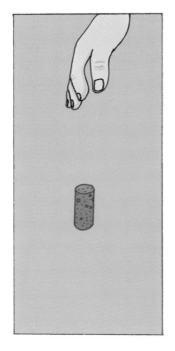

Test this cork against a
cork without paper.
Drop them at the same
time to make it fair.

What is different about
the way the two corks
fall through the air?
Does it make any difference
if you turn the cork so that
the paper is at the bottom?

Sometimes we want things
to come down slowly
through the air.
Parachutes are used to
bring people down safely
from airplanes.

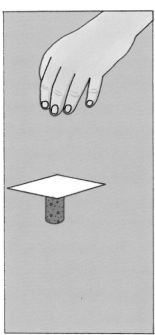

How to make your own parachute

You need ★ a plastic bag
          ★ 4 pieces of string

★ a small toy to be the
   parachute person
★ tape

Cut out a square of plastic.
Tape one piece of string to
each corner of the square.
Ask an adult to help you
hold the ends together and
tie them in a knot.
Tie the parachute person
to the ends of the string.
Throw it up in the air.
Does it float down?

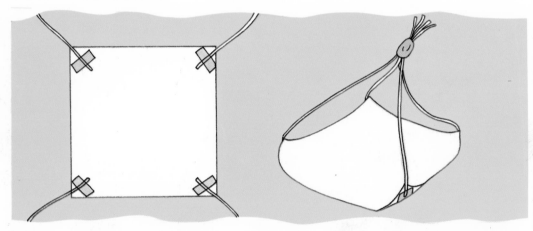

Give the parachute person
a pack to carry.
You could use a blob of
clay to put on the
back of the toy.
Is this pack going to change
the way the parachute
comes down?
Throw the parachute up
again and see what happens.

What happens when you push things through the air?

Get a large piece of cardboard. Hold it at the bottom corners with both hands. Now run as fast as you can into the wind. Is it easy to run with the card like this? What can you feel as you push forward?

Try holding the card so that the edge points into the wind.

Which is the best way to hold the card so that it goes through the air easily?

When you pushed the card like this
air could pass over it smoothly.

What do you notice about these
flying things?

They are all pointed at the front.
This helps them get through the air.

How to make your own spinner

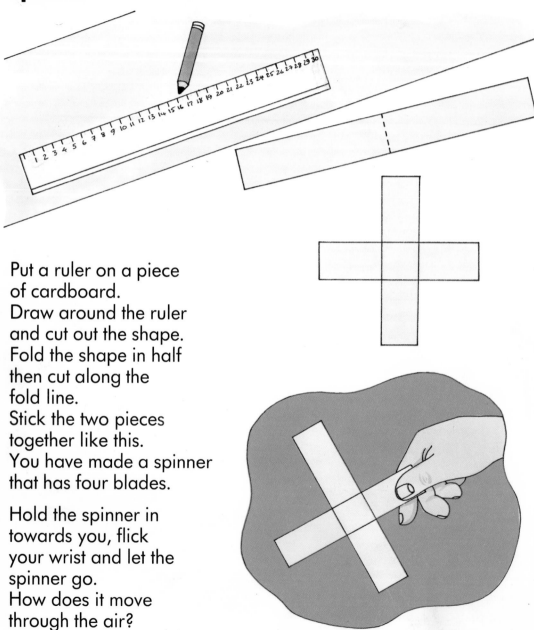

Put a ruler on a piece of cardboard.
Draw around the ruler and cut out the shape.
Fold the shape in half then cut along the fold line.
Stick the two pieces together like this.
You have made a spinner that has four blades.

Hold the spinner in towards you, flick your wrist and let the spinner go.
How does it move through the air?

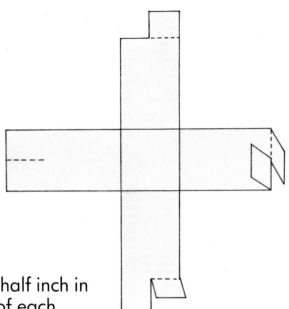

Measure one-half inch in
from the end of each
blade and draw a line.
Cut up the middle of
each blade to this line.
Now your spinner has
some flaps.

Turn the spinner around in
your hand and pull up the
first flap on each blade.
Flick your spinner
through the air.
Does it move in a straight
line or a curved line?

Try changing the flaps
up and down.
Does this change the
way the spinner moves?

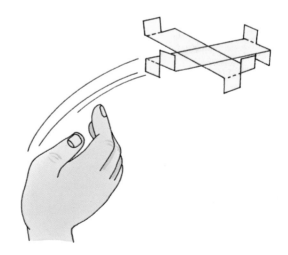

How to make a glider

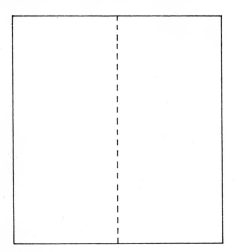

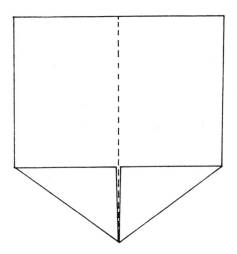

Get a piece of paper.
Fold it in half.
Then open it up.

Fold the two top corners
into the middle so that they
touch.

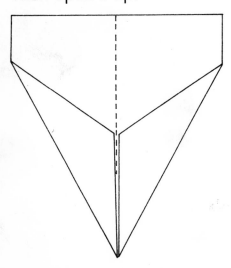

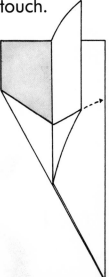

Fold these corners in again
so that they meet along the
middle fold.

Fold the glider in half again.
Bend the back pieces down
to make the wings.

How to launch a glider

When you launch a flying thing,
it means you are
sending it through the air.
Put your hand underneath
the glider, about half
way down.
Lift your arm up high
behind your head.
Point the nose of the
glider downwards.
Launch it gently into
the air.
How far does it fly?

Would a small glider fly as far as a large one?

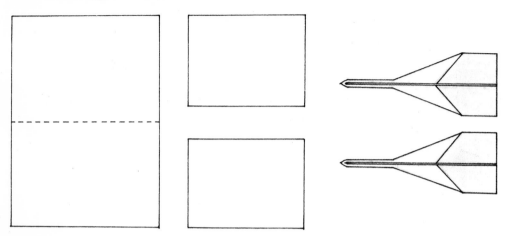

Get the same size paper as
before.
Fold it and cut it in half.
Make a glider from each half
of the paper.
Test the large glider and
one small glider.
Which one flies the farthest?

Would a heavy glider fly as far as a light one?

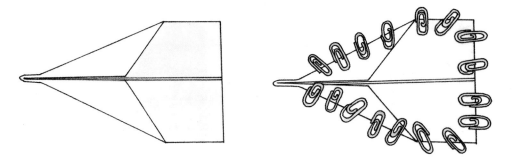

Get the two small gliders.
How could you make one heavier
than the other?
You could add some paper clips
to one glider.
Which glider do you think will
fly the farthest?
Try it and see.

How to make a Hurricane Glider

You need ★ a flat stick
(an old ruler will do)
★ oaktag
★ tape
★ clay

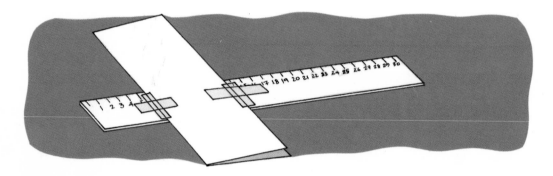

Get a piece of oaktag and fold it in half.
Tape it across your stick to make the wings.
Cut two pieces of card to make the tail.

Fold each piece in half and tape them together. (Look at the drawing below.) Tape the tail onto the glider.

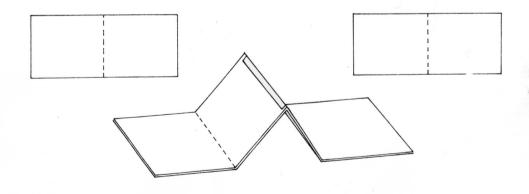

A new glider or airplane
has to be tested to see
how well it flies.
This is called the test flight.
Give your glider a test flight.

What could you do
to make it fly farther?
Would it help if you made the
wings into a curved shape?

Look at the shape of
a bird's wing.

Would it help if you made the nose
of the glider heavier
with a blob of clay?
Test it and see.

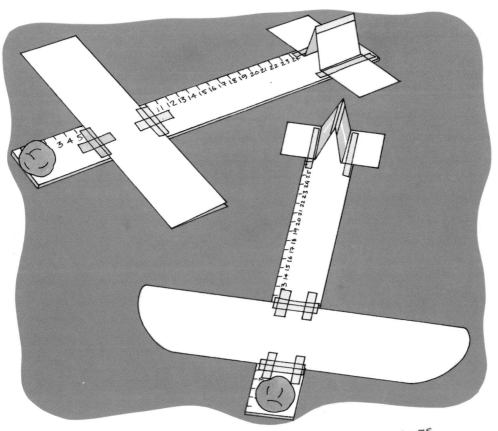

Airplanes need an engine
to make them fly through
the air.
A Jumbo jet is a large
airplane with jet
engines.
Here is an experiment to
show you how a jet engine
pushes an airplane forward.

You need ★ some long balloons
        ★ a balloon pump
        ★ a piece of thin string
        ★ a straw
        ★ a bulldog clip
        ★ tape

Thread the string
through the straw.
Ask two friends to hold
the string.
Use a balloon pump to
blow up a balloon.
Fasten the neck of the balloon
with a bulldog clip.
Tape the balloon to the
straw like this.

The balloon is full of air.
What will happen when you
take off the bulldog clip?
Try it and see.

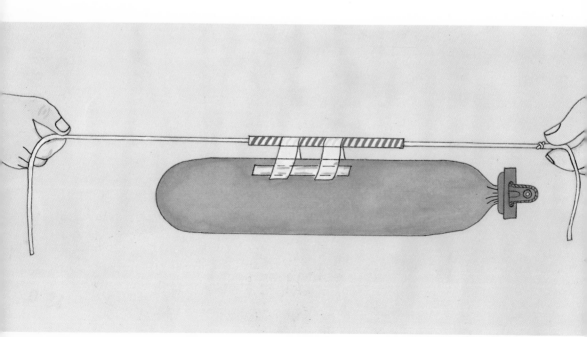

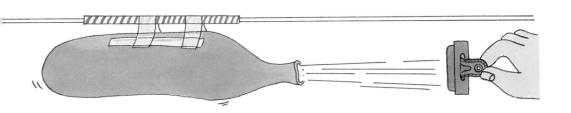

Which way does the
balloon go?
Which way does the air
come out?
The air rushes out at
the back, and the balloon
is pushed forward.
A jet engine makes hot
gases rush out at the
back of the airplane.
This pushes the airplane
forward through the air.

Here is a new card game.
Get some small pieces of cardboard.
On each card draw a picture
of something that moves in the air.
Read across and down the grid.
Put the cards in the right boxes.

	engine	no engine
wings		
no wings		

Look at the things which have
no engine and no wings.
How do they get up into the air?
Sort the cards into these sets.

no engine

no wings

1. A set of things which need to be thrown
   or pushed up into the air.

2. A set of things which need to be taken up
   by airplane.

3. A set of things which only need the wind
   to lift them.

Keep looking out for things
which move in the air.
Draw each one on a piece of cardboard
and use it in the game.

Index

Airplane 25, 26, 27

Balloon 26, 27

Bridle 10

Glider 20, 21, 22, 23

Hurricane glider 24, 25

Jet engine 26, 27

Kite 7, 8, 9, 10, 11

Parachute 14, 15

Spinner 18, 19

Test flight 25

Towing line 10

1 2 3 4 5 6 7 8 9 10—JDL—93 92 91 90 89 88 87 86 85